GREATEST OF ALL TIME COLLEGE SPORTS

G.O.A.T. COLLEGE WOMEN'S BASKETBALL TEAMS

Diane Lindsey Reeves

Lerner Publications ◆ Minneapolis

Special thanks to my favorite college women's basketball fans, Gayle Lindsey Bryan and Hollis Grace Palmer.

Stats in this book are accurate through the 2023–2024 women's college basketball season.

Lerner Publications Company
An imprint of Lerner Publishing Group, Inc.
241 First Avenue North
Minneapolis, MN 55401 USA

For reading levels and more information, look up this title at www.lernerbooks.com.

Main body text set in Aptifer Sans LT Pro.
Typeface provided by Linotype.

Library of Congress Cataloging-in-Publication Data

Names: Reeves, Diane Lindsey, 1959–author.
Title: G.O.A.T. college women's basketball teams / Diane Lindsey Reeves.
Other titles: Greatest-of-all-time college women's basketball teams
Description: Minneapolis : Lerner Publications, 2026. | Series: Lerner sports. Greatest of all time college sports | Includes bibliographical references and index. | Audience: Ages 7–11 | Audience: Grades 2–3 | Summary: "The greatest college women's basketball teams have thrilled fans with incredible games, superstar players, and jaw-dropping winning streaks. Meet the players and coaches that make it all possible, and then create your own top-ten list"—Provided by publisher.
Identifiers: LCCN 2024044930 (print) | LCCN 2024044931 (ebook) | ISBN 9798765668603 (library binding) | ISBN 9798765684221 (paperback) | ISBN 9798765677933 (epub)
Subjects: LCSH: Basketball teams—United States—Juvenile literature. | Women basketball players—United States—Juvenile literature. | College sports—United States—Juvenile literature.
Classification: LCC GV885.7 .R44 2026 (print) | LCC GV885.7 (ebook) | DDC 796.323—dc23/eng/20250116

LC record available at https://lccn.loc.gov/2024044930
LC ebook record available at https://lccn.loc.gov/2024044931

Manufactured in the United States of America
1-1011971-53828-4/24/2025

TABLE OF CONTENTS

Caitlin Clark takes a shot during the final game of the 2024 national women's college basketball tournament.

Women Take the Court

University of Iowa superstar Caitlin Clark dribbled the ball. She made a quick move to step behind the three-point line. Clark jumped and shot the ball. *Swish!*

The game on April 7, 2024, was the title game of the National Collegiate Athletic Association (NCAA) women's basketball tournament. The unbeaten University of South Carolina Gamecocks were up against the Iowa Hawkeyes. This was Iowa superstar Caitlin Clark's last game as a college player. It was her final chance to win a national title.

More than 24 million fans watched the Gamecocks win 87–75. It was the most viewers ever for a women's college basketball game. Men's college basketball teams often draw more fans and media attention. But fewer than 15 million people watched the men's title game that year.

South Carolina Gamecocks players and coaches celebrate their 2024 NCAA championship win against Iowa.

FACTS AT A GLANCE

- A great lineup of coaches leads college women's basketball. They include Geno Auriemma, Kim Mulkey, and Dawn Staley.
- Some college basketball players join the WNBA after they leave school. Among the top players to go from college to the WNBA are Brittney Griner, Cynthia Cooper-Duke, Sylvia Fowles, and Seimone Augustus.
- Games between rival teams are some of the most exciting for fans. The Louisiana State University (LSU) Tigers and South Carolina Gamecocks are big rivals. So are the Stanford Cardinal and University of Connecticut (UConn) Huskies.
- UConn is the winningest college women's basketball team of all time.

This level of success was a long time coming for college women's basketball. The first women's college game was played in 1899. Yet the Olympic Games didn't include women's basketball until 1976. Men's basketball became an Olympic sport in 1936.

Women's basketball took another step forward when the Women's National Basketball Association (WNBA) began in 1996. It gave women a chance to take the game pro. WNBA teams dazzle their many fans with exiting games and talented players.

Read on to learn about some of the greatest of all time (G.O.A.T.) women's college basketball teams. They have all had success over a long period of time. Each team has won at least one NCAA title. They have a track record of wins, amazing players, and terrific coaches.

You may or may not agree with all the team rankings in this book. No problem! You'll get to choose your own G.O.A.T. teams at the end.

When rivals such as Duke and North Carolina meet on the court, players fight hard to win.

NO. 10

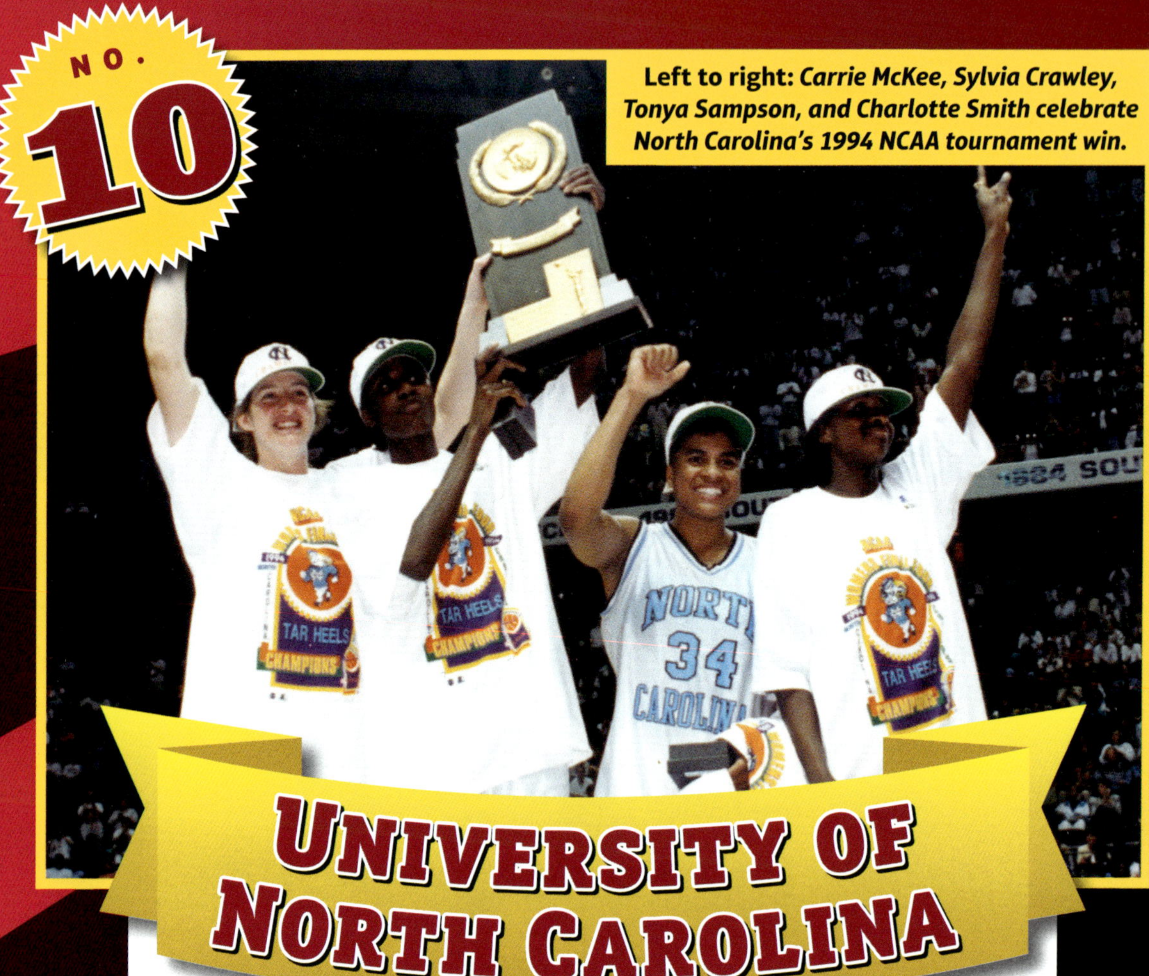

Left to right: ***Carrie McKee, Sylvia Crawley, Tonya Sampson, and Charlotte Smith celebrate North Carolina's 1994 NCAA tournament win.***

University of North Carolina

It's been awhile since the University of North Carolina (UNC) women last won the NCAA title. But diehard UNC Tar Heels fans will never forget the 1994 season. Just as the final buzzer sounded to end the title game, Charlotte Smith nailed a three-point shot! UNC edged out Louisiana Tech in a 60–59 victory.

Smith later became the women's coach at Elon University. She remembers the buzzer-beating moment well. She said winning the title was the result of months of hard work and learning to play as a team.

The UNC women's team has piled up 954 wins since its start in 1971. They have captured four regular-season Atlantic Coast Conference (ACC) titles. They have also won the ACC tournament nine times.

The team showed what it's made of in 2024 with a big win. The Louisville Cardinals ranked higher and were expected to win. But UNC's Deja Kelly led her team by making 14 out of 16 free throws. The Tar Heels won 88–79!

UNC's Lexi Donarski* (left) *fights for the ball in a game against Duke in 2020.

UNC TAR HEELS FACTS

- Many UNC women have been drafted by WNBA teams. They include Ivory Latta, Paris Kea, Jessica Breland, and Nikki Teasley.
- UNC's neighbor Duke University is UNC's biggest rival. UNC leads the matchup with a 54–53 record against Duke.
- The UNC women's basketball team first played in 1971. Since then, they have played in the NCAA tournament 31 times.
- Like most great coaches, UNC coach Courtney Banghart was a player first. She played for Dartmouth College. Banghart stood out by making 273 three-point baskets in her Dartmouth career.

NO. 9

Angel Reese (right) in action against the Miami Hurricanes in 2023

LOUISIANA STATE UNIVERSITY

The LSU Tigers took out Iowa in the 2023 NCAA title game with a record-breaking score of 102-85. It was the first title win for the team. But it was the fourth for their new coach, Kim Mulkey. She also had three title wins during her years coaching Baylor.

Three of women's basketball's greatest players were LSU Tigers. Angel Reese led the team to their 2023 title. She scored an impressive 1,443 points in two seasons with the team. She also snatched 996 rebounds.

Center Sylvia Fowles made it to the NCAA Final Four all four years of her college career. She set team records with 1,570 rebounds and 321 blocks. The Chicago Sky chose her with the second overall pick in the 2008 WNBA draft.

Semione Augustus in action against Tennessee in 2004

In high school, it was obvious that Seimone Augustus was a standout player. A *Sports Illustrated for Women* headline even suggested she was the next Michael Jordan. Some say Augustus put the LSU team on the map. She was a scoring and rebounding machine. She later played in the WNBA and won three Olympic gold medals with Team USA.

LSU TIGERS FACTS

- The Tigers are no strangers to NCAA tournaments. They have played in six Final Four games.
- Fowles (number 34) and Augustus (number 33) had their jersey numbers retired by LSU. To honor them, no other LSU player will wear those numbers.
- Mulkey is one of the best coaches in college women's basketball. She signed a huge 10-year, $36 million contract with LSU. That's more money than any other NCAA women's coach earns.

NO. 8

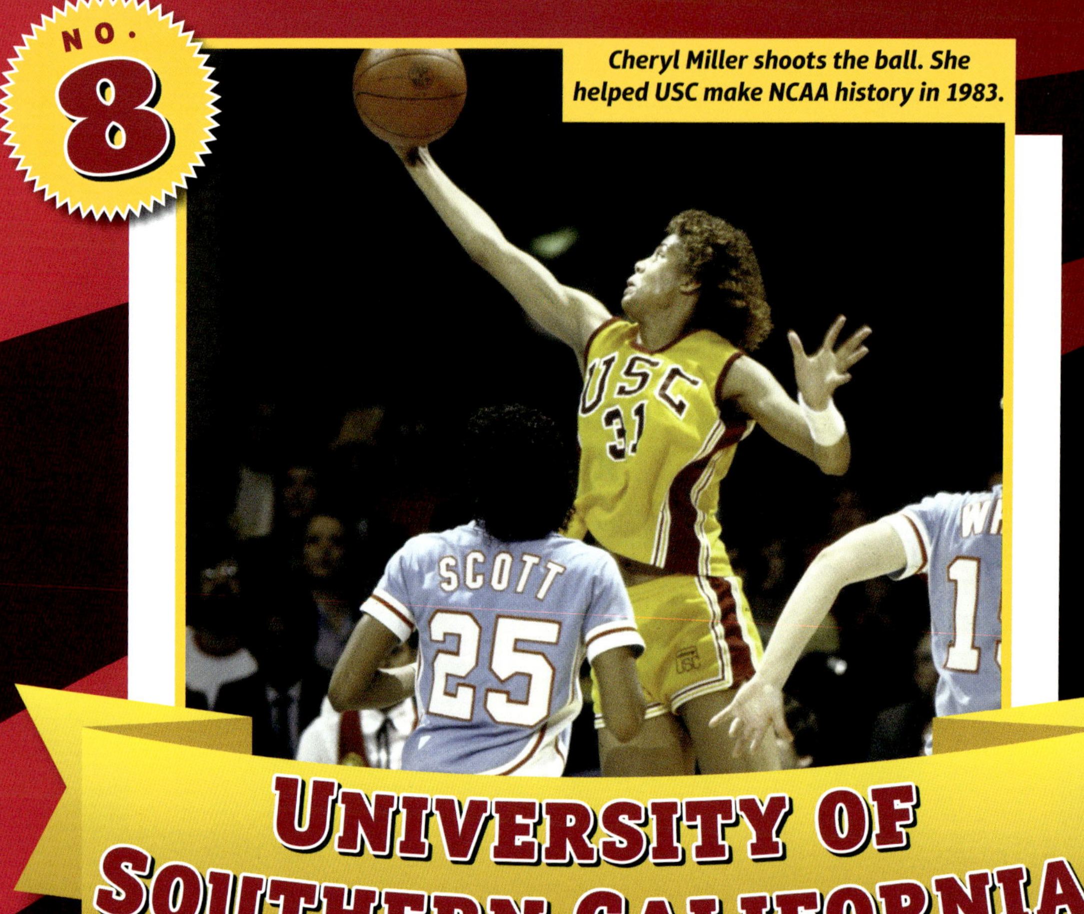

Cheryl Miller shoots the ball. She helped USC make NCAA history in 1983.

UNIVERSITY OF SOUTHERN CALIFORNIA

The University of Southern California (USC) Trojans' winning ways started in 1982. That's when they made it to the NCAA tournament's Elite Eight, the round that comes before the Final Four. Then, in 1983 and 1984, the Trojans won back-to-back NCAA championships.

The Trojans made basketball history in 1983. They won the NCAA championship with the first starting lineup of all Black players. The team's starting lineup included Cynthia Cooper, Cheryl Miller, Pamela and Paula McGee, and Rhonda Windham.

Head coach Lindsay Gottlieb joined USC in 2021. Before USC, she had been the first female assistant coach for the National Basketball Association (NBA) Cleveland Cavaliers. She has helped the Trojans return to the top of women's college basketball.

In 2024, USC won the Pac-12 Conference title. It was a huge win against top-ranked Stanford. The win bumped the Trojans up to third in the national rankings. It was USC's best ranking in 38 years.

McKenzie Forbes celebrates a big win in the 2024 Pac-12 championship game.

USC TROJANS FACTS

- In high school, Cheryl Miller scored 105 points in one game! She broke a US national record. She was also the first woman to make a slam dunk in a college game.
- Pamela McGee was a first-round draft pick in the WNBA's first season. She is also the first WNBA player to have a son play for the NBA.
- *Women of Troy*, an HBO film, tells the story of the Trojans' 1980s success.
- Cynthia Cooper, a famous USC player in the 1980s, coached USC from 2013 to 2017.

No. 7

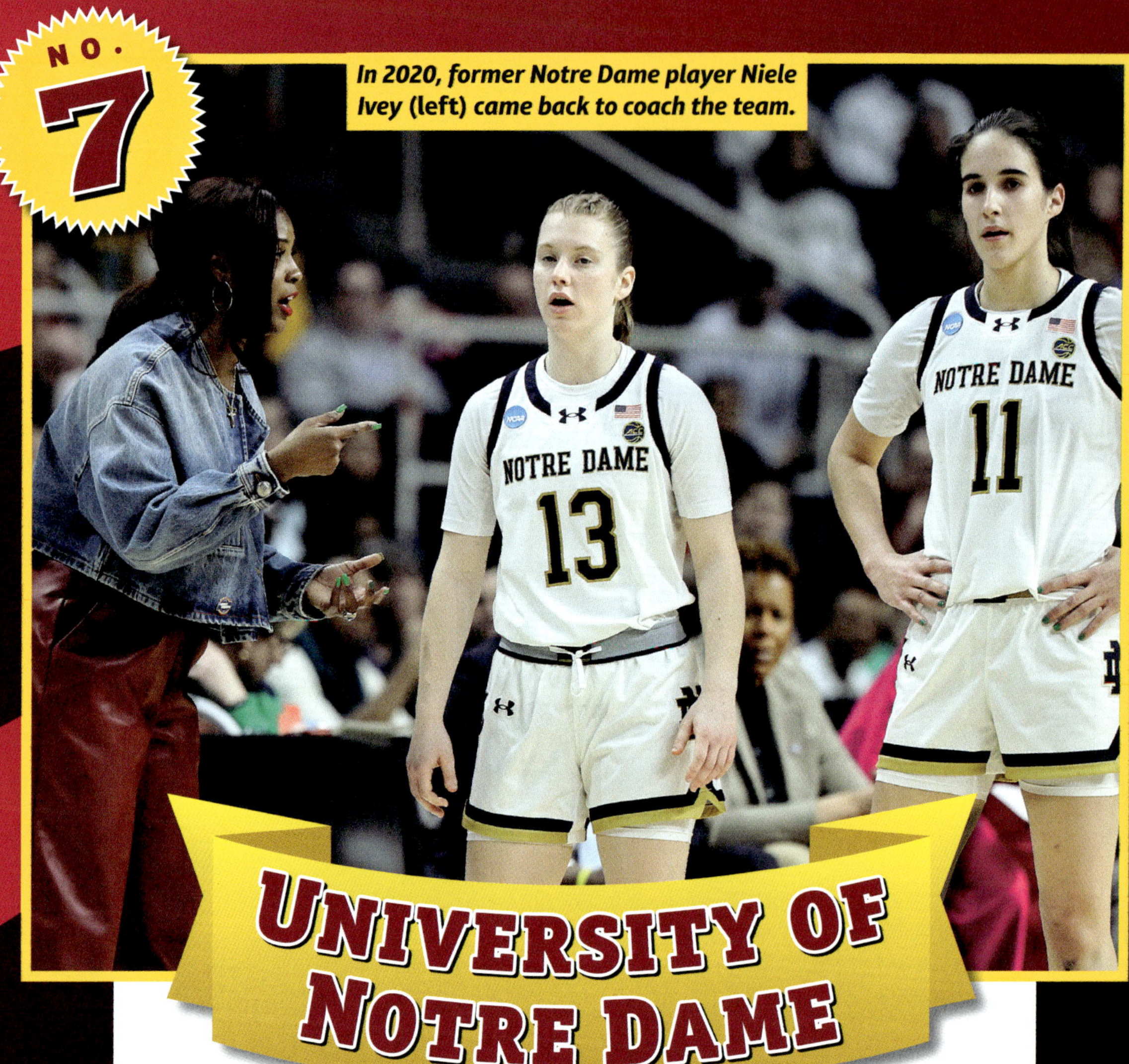

In 2020, former Notre Dame player Niele Ivey (left) came back to coach the team.

University of Notre Dame

The Notre Dame women's basketball team is a two-time NCAA champ. Notre Dame won the title in 2001 and again in 2018. Then they came close to winning a repeat championship in 2019. They lost a heartbreaking game by one point, 82–81, against Baylor.

It's been several years since the team has won a national title. But they've been winning in other ways. Notre Dame has been conference champs six times. They've played in nine Final Fours.

Over the past 25 years, they've won at least 20 games each year.

All that winning was the result of great players and coaches. Muffet McGraw led the team to both of Notre Dame's national championships during her 33 years as head coach. A dream team of the five top Notre Dame players of all time would include Arike Ogunbowale, Jewell Loyd, Brianna Turner, Ruth Riley, and Alicia Ratay.

Arike Ogunbowale makes a move to the basket.

NOTRE DAME FIGHTING IRISH FACTS

- From 1981 to 2024, the team had 1,042 wins and only 345 losses.
- Twenty Fighting Irish women have been drafted by WNBA teams. Two—Jewell Loyd and Jackie Young—were the number one overall picks.
- Niele Ivey played for Notre Dame when they won the 2001 NCAA championship. She came back as head coach in 2020.
- Arike Ogunbowale is Notre Dame's top women's basketball scorer. She scored 2,626 points.

NO. 6

Brittney Griner (top) blocks a shot against Notre Dame.

BAYLOR UNIVERSITY

The Baylor Bears women's basketball team has seen some highs and lows. Kim Mulkey took over as head coach in 2000. She came to the rescue after a tough year when the team had seven wins and 20 losses. They ranked at the bottom of the Big 12 Conference.

Mulkey rallied the team to some of their greatest victories. They include three NCAA national titles in 2005, 2012, and 2019.

The 2012 win capped a perfect season of 40–0!

Coach Nicki Collen took over the team in 2021, and they continue to rack up impressive wins. They also keep appearing in the NCAA tournament. They've had big wins over tough opponents such as Utah. They closed out the 2024 season with 26 wins.

Mulkey was a tough act to follow. But Collen keeps moving the Bears in the right direction. Their record of success makes them one of the best teams in NCAA history.

US president Barack Obama* (front row left) *celebrates the Baylor Bears' 40–0 season with the team in 2012.

BAYLOR BEARS FACTS

- Kim Mulkey was the first woman to win NCAA national championships as both a player and coach.
- Center Brittney Griner is one of the Bears' most famous players. She racked up 3,293 points, 1,305 rebounds, 748 blocks, and 18 slam dunks. That's more slam dunks than any other college women's basketball player in history.
- The WNBA has drafted 24 Baylor players, including 11 as first-round picks.
- Only Tennessee and UConn have more national titles than Baylor has.

NO. 5

Aliyah Boston (right) was picked first overall by the Indiana Fever during the 2023 WNBA draft.

UNIVERSITY OF SOUTH CAROLINA

Basketball doesn't get any better than it did for the South Carolina Gamecocks in 2024. They finished the regular season with a perfect 33–0 record. They scored and defended their way to the final game of the NCAA tournament.

Iowa's Caitlin Clark scored 30 points against South Carolina in the title game. But the Gamecocks won by a score of 87–75. Winning the title was the ultimate revenge for South Carolina. Iowa had beaten the Gamecocks in the 2023 NCAA tournament.

This was South Carolina's third NCAA title under coach Dawn Staley. They also won in 2017 and 2022. Winning is something

Staley does well. Her team has racked up many conference title wins and has had amazing success against college basketball's best teams.

South Carolina continues to produce skilled players. Sixteen former Gamecocks have joined the WNBA so far. Aliyah Boston was named WNBA Rookie of the Year in 2023. Hopes are high for this basketball superpower to keep winning and producing great players.

Dawn Staley* (center) *is an award-winning former player and coach.

SOUTH CAROLINA GAMECOCKS FACTS

- The South Carolina women's team was first called the Pullets, or young hens. Then they became the Carolina Chicks. In 1977, they changed to Lady Gamecocks. They later changed again to Gamecocks.
- Center Kamilla Cardoso scored 15 points and grabbed 15 rebounds in the 2024 title game. Later that year, the Chicago Sky chose her with the third overall pick in the WNBA draft.
- In 2024, the Gamecocks joined a group of only five women's college teams that have celebrated perfect seasons. The others are Baylor, UConn, Tennessee, and Texas.

NO. 4

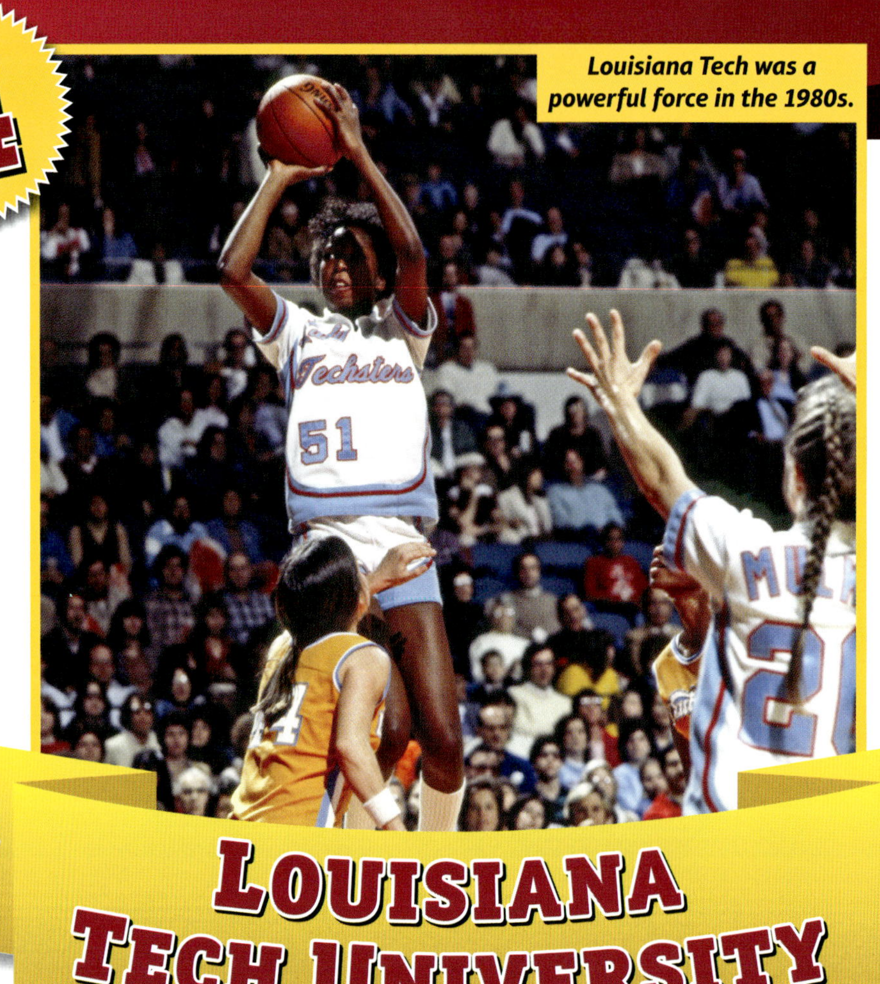

Louisiana Tech was a powerful force in the 1980s.

LOUISIANA TECH UNIVERSITY

The Louisiana Tech Techsters are pioneers in women's college basketball. They started strong in 1974 with Women's Basketball Hall of Fame coach Sonja Hogg. The team got better every year. Louisiana Tech became one of the best women's college basketball teams in the US.

In the early 1980s, the Techsters were almost unstoppable. They had a winning streak of 54 games before losing to Old Dominion in a 61–58 heartbreaker. Louisiana Tech bounced back from the loss to win 15 more games in a row.

And they didn't just win, they won big. In their 1982 season, the Techsters won 35 games by an average of 33 points. In 11 of those games, they scored more than 100 points. They topped it all by winning the first NCAA women's basketball title.

In recent years, the Techsters haven't had as much success as they once did. But the team is still celebrated for its history and its impact on women's college basketball.

Kim Mulkey played for Louisiana Tech from 1981 to 1984. She later became the head coach of Baylor and LSU.

LOUISIANA TECH TECHSTERS FACTS

- Women's Basketball Hall of Fame coach Kim Mulkey was a point guard for the team from 1981 to 1984. She competed in four Final Fours and won two national titles.
- Louisiana Tech has advanced to the Final Four 13 times.
- Brooke Stoehr became the Techsters head coach in 2016. She played basketball at Louisiana Tech from 1998 to 2002.
- The Techsters have had many successful players. They include five Olympic medal winners, eight Women's Basketball Hall of Famers, and 21 WNBA players.

NO. 3

Tara VanDerveer (center) retired in 2024 as the winningest coach in NCAA history.

STANFORD UNIVERSITY

When Tara VanDerveer told her father she was taking the head coaching job at Stanford in 1985, he warned her that it was impossible to win there. The team didn't have a long history of success. She took the job anyway. When she retired 38 years later, she had proven her father wrong.

VanDerveer led the Stanford Cardinal to three NCAA national championships and two second-place finishes. They were a Pac-12 Conference powerhouse. VanDerveer made Stanford one of the top women's basketball schools in the US. By the time she retired in 2024, VanDerveer had won more basketball games than any other men's or women's college coach in history.

Stanford's team attracts top-tier players. So far, 31 Cardinal players have been drafted into the WNBA. They include Cameron Brink, who was chosen with the second overall pick by the Los Angeles Sparks in the 2024 draft.

Cameron Brink grabs a rebound against the UCLA Bruins.

STANFORD CARDINAL FACTS

- The Cardinal often play in the NCAA tournament. They've played in 15 Final Fours and 22 Elite Eights.
- Stanford played in the very first women's college basketball game. They took on the University of California in 1896 and won 2–1.
- Since 1981, Stanford has won 1,145 games and lost 289.
- The Ogwumike sisters are two of Stanford's best players of all time. Nneka Ogwumike went on to have a very successful pro career with the Los Angeles Sparks. Chiney Ogwumike became the first Black woman to host a national show for ESPN.

Head coach Pat Summitt (right) and her son Tyler celebrate Tennessee's 2007 NCAA title win.

University of Tennessee

Tennessee's Lady Volunteers (Vols) have won eight NCAA titles. Only UConn has won more. The Lady Vols were unstoppable in the 1990s with three back-to-back titles in 1996, 1997, and 1998.

Much of the credit for the team's success goes to their former coach, Pat Summit. She was one of the most successful NCAA coaches ever. She coached Tennessee for 38 years and never had a losing season. When she retired in 2012, her teams had won an amazing 84 percent of their games.

In recent years, the team has been on another winning streak. They won 25 regular-season games in both the 2021–2022 and 2022–2023 seasons. With new coach Kim Caldwell, the Lady Vols are in a good position to keep up their winning ways.

Jordan Walker and the 2022–2023 Lady Vols team won 25 regular-season games.

TENNESSEE LADY VOLUNTEERS FACTS

- Pat Summit was named the Naismith Basketball Coach of the Century in 2000. In 2012, US president Barack Obama awarded her the Presidential Medal of Freedom, one of the nation's highest honors.
- The Lady Vols were national champs in 1987, 1989, 1991, 1996, 1997, 1998, 2007, and 2008.
- Women's basketball has been an official sport at the University of Tennessee since 1920.
- Tennessee is the only women's basketball team to have played in all 42 NCAA tournaments since 1982.

NO. 1

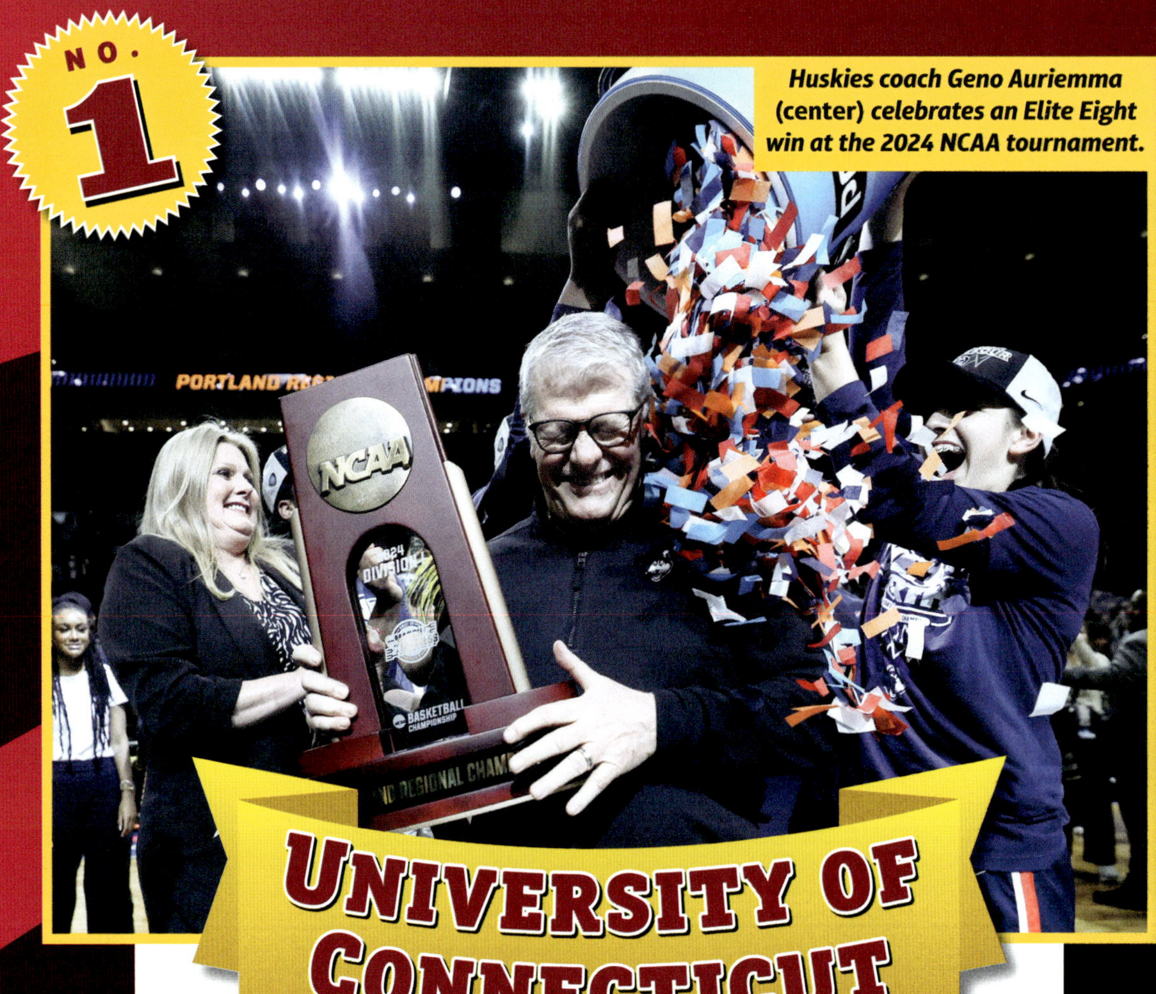

Huskies coach Geno Auriemma (center) celebrates an Elite Eight win at the 2024 NCAA tournament.

University of Connecticut

The UConn Huskies are the winningest women's college basketball team of all time. They have 11 NCAA championships and 23 Final Four appearances. One of the best coaches in history, Geno Auriemma, has led the team since 1985. Often named coach of the year, he has built the most successful women's team in the nation.

Along with their NCAA wins, the team has had six perfect seasons with no losses. They've won a whopping 59 conference titles. The Huskies have racked up 1,241 wins. With only 312 losses, they win almost 80 percent of their games!

High school basketball players from all over the country dream of playing for UConn. Those skilled enough to make the team go through tough training that prepares them to compete at the highest level. That's why UConn is the women's college basketball G.O.A.T.

Breanna Stewart takes a shot against the Maryland Terrapins.

UCONN HUSKIES FACTS

- From 2014 to 2017, the Huskies made women's basketball history with a 111-game winning streak.
- UConn has more number-one overall WNBA draft picks than any other college. They are Sue Bird in 2002, Diana Taurasi in 2004, Tina Charles in 2010, Maya Moore in 2011, and Breanna Stewart in 2016.
- The Huskies made NCAA history by winning four national championships in a row from 2013 to 2016.
- The Huskies had two back-to-back perfect seasons in 2009 and 2010.

YOUR G.O.A.T.

Now it's your turn to put together your own list of G.O.A.T. women's college basketball teams. What facts will you consider when you make your list? What is important to you as a fan?

The teams in this book are ranked largely by the number of national championships they have won. How many titles a team has is an important factor when choosing a G.O.A.T. in any sport. Each team's overall record is another thing to consider, as well as their average points per game. How many Final Four appearances has a team made? What stars of the past and present have played for the team?

Grab a pen and a sheet of paper and make you G.O.A.T. list. Do any of your picks match the teams featured in this book? It's your list. You decide!

WOMEN'S COLLEGE BASKETBALL FACTS

- In January 2024, Grambling State University won the biggest blowout in women's NCAA history. It was a landslide victory against the College of Biblical Studies Ambassadors. The score was 150–18.
- In January 2024, Tara VanDerveer became the winningest men's or women's coach in college basketball history. She retired after the 2024 NCAA tournament with 1,216 career wins.
- More fans show up to cheer on the South Carolina Gamecocks than any other college women's team. An average of 13,239 fans attend their games.
- Sports fans paid big bucks to watch the 2024 women's Final Four games at Rocket Mortgage Fieldhouse in Cleveland, Ohio. Some tickets were sold for as much as $1,000. It was the most expensive women's Final Four ever.

GLOSSARY

conference: a group of teams that play against one another

draft: when teams take turns choosing new players

Final Four: the last four teams competing in the NCAA national tournament

free throw: an open shot taken from behind a set line after a foul by an opponent

National Collegiate Athletic Association (NCAA): the group that oversees college sports in the US

rebound: taking control of the ball after a missed shot

rival: a player or team that tries to defeat or be more successful than another

slam dunk: a shot in basketball made by jumping high into the air and throwing the ball down through the basket

title: championship

three-point shot: a shot taken from behind the three-point line on the court

LEARN MORE

Brittanica Kids: Basketball
https://kids.britannica.com/kids/article/basketball/352831

Doeden, Matt. *G.O.A.T. Women's Basketball Teams.* Minneapolis: Lerner Publications, 2021.

Huddleston, Emma. *Legends of Women's Basketball.* Mendota Heights, MN: Press Box Books, 2021.

Kiddle: Women's Basketball Facts for Kids
https://kids.kiddle.co/Women%27s_basketball

Labrecque, Ellen. *All-Time Best WNBA Players.* Mankato, MN: The Child's World, 2020.

Wonderopolis: What Is March Madness?
https://www.wonderopolis.org/wonder/what-is-march-madness

INDEX

PHOTO ACKNOWLEDGMENTS

Interior; EFKS/Shutterstock, Interior; robertsrob/iStock, Interior; 9859873_183/iStock, Interior; yummybuum/Shutterstock, Interior; Alex Voylokov/Shutterstock, p. 4; Ben Solomon/Getty, p. 5; C. Morgan Engel/Getty, p. 7; Icon Sportswire/Getty, p. 8; Dana Gelin/UNC Athletics, p. 9; Dana Gelin/UNC Athletics, p. 10; Kevin C. Cox/Getty, p. 11; Bill Frakes/Getty, p. 12; Jerry Wachter/Getty, p. 13; Candice Ward/Getty, p. 14; Andy Lyons/Getty, p. 15; Icon Sportswire/Getty, p. 16; Justin Edmonds/Getty; p. 17; Chip Somodevilla/Getty, p. 18; Sarah Stier/Getty, p. 19; Sean Rayford/Getty, p. 20; George Tiedemann/Getty, p. 21; Jerry Wachter/Getty; p. 22; Thearon W. Henderson/Getty, p. 23; Theron W. Henderson, p. 24; Jim McIssac/Getty, p. 25; Eakin Howard/Getty, p. 26; Tyler Schank/Getty, p. 27; G Fiume/Getty.

Cover: Erica Denhoff/AP.